MathStart®
TALLYING

Tally O'Malley

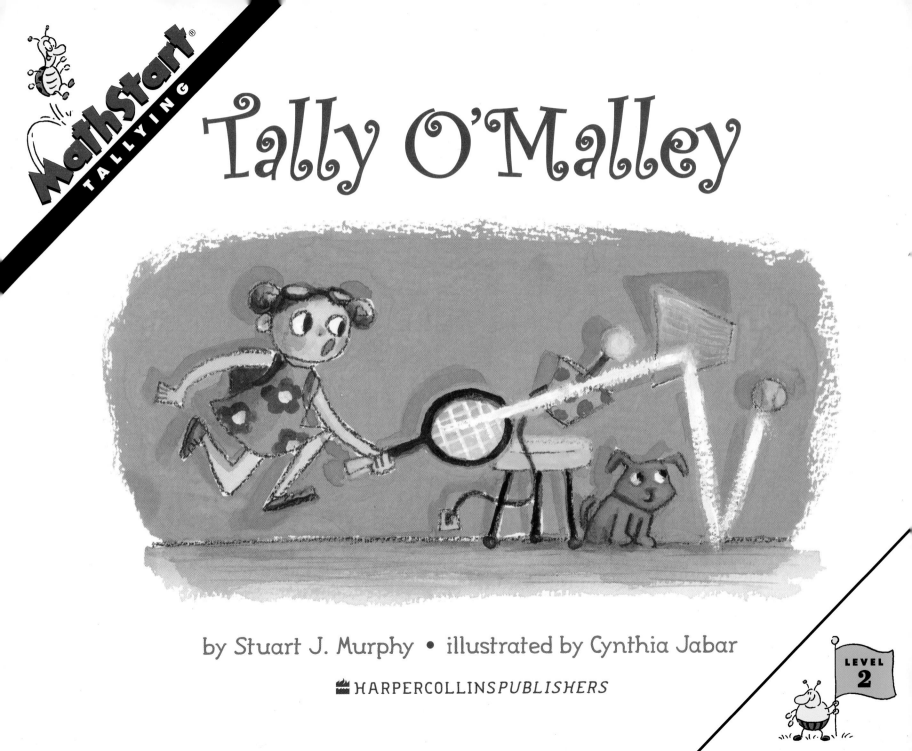

by Stuart J. Murphy • illustrated by Cynthia Jabar

HARPERCOLLINSPUBLISHERS

LEVEL
2

To Maureen Kelly Murphy and
the Irish side of our family
—S.J.M.

For my lovely family.
Squabbles: 4723, love, infinite.
—C.J.

The publisher and author would like to thank teachers Patricia Chase,
Phyllis Goldman, and Patrick Hopfensperger for their help in making
the math in MathStart just right for kids.

HarperCollins®, ✦®, and MathStart® are registered trademarks of HarperCollins Publishers.
For more information about the MathStart series, write to HarperCollins Children's Books,
1350 Avenue of the Americas, New York, NY 10019,
or visit our website at www.mathstartbooks.com.

Bugs incorporated in the MathStart series design were painted by Jon Buller.

Library of Congress Cataloging-in-Publication Data
Murphy, Stuart J.
  Tally O'Malley / by Stuart J. Murphy ; illustrated by Cynthia
Jabar.— 1st ed.
p. cm. — (MathStart)
"Level 2. Tallying"
Summary: On a car trip to the beach, the O'Malley family
children compete by playing games together.
  ISBN 0-06-053162-2 — ISBN 0-06-053164-9 (pbk.)
  [1. Games for travelers—Fiction. 2. Automobile travel—Fiction.]
I. Jabar, Cynthia, ill. II. Title. III. Series.
PZ7.M9563Tal 2004
[E]—dc22
2003017619

Typography by Elynn Cohen
1 2 3 4 5 6 7 8 9 10
❖ First Edition

Tally O'Malley

The O'Malleys were ready to go on vacation.
Almost ready, that is.

"Did you pack the beach towels?" asked Dad.

"Did you lock the back door?" asked Mom.

"C'mon, Shamrock, get in!" ordered Eric,
pulling on the dog's leash.

"I can't find my sunglasses!" said Nell.

4

5

Finally they were on their way.

They had been on the road for almost three hours

when Eric grumbled, "Aren't we ever going to get there?"

"Ick! Shamrock's breathing on me!" said Bridget.

"I can't find my baseball hat!" said Nell.

"Why don't we play a tally game?" asked Mom.

First they had to decide on something to count.

"Let's do cars," said Eric. He loved tally games
because he almost always won.

"Okay," Mom agreed. "Pick your colors."

"I take silver," said Eric.

"I take blue," said Bridget. "How about you, Nell?"

"Red," answered Nell. Red was her favorite color.

Eric laughed. "You always pick red and you never win," he said.

9

Mom handed out paper and pencils.

"Do you remember how to play, Nell?" asked Bridget.
"When you see a red car, you make a tally mark.

|

Then make another one for each red car you see.
When you're up to three, it will look like this:

|||

When you get to five, you make a little bundle so they're
easy to count."

||||

"This will be a twenty-minute game," explained Mom.
"Ready! Set! Go!"

"There's a silver one," said Eric immediately. "And two more over there."

"I see a blue one," said Bridget. "And another one right behind it."

"Ha! I see a red one," said Nell.

"Nell, there's another," said Dad.

"No helping!" yelled Eric.

"Time's up!" said Mom,
just as they pulled into
a rest stop for lunch.

Dad took Shamrock
for a walk while they
counted up their tally marks.
"I win!" Eric shouted. "I always win."

"You get to wear the tally medal," said Mom. The medal was really a plastic shamrock that Dad had given the dog on her first birthday.

"You think you're so great," whined Bridget. "Tally O'Malley!"

17

The line for hamburgers was very long.

"I'm hungry," said Bridget.

"I want ice cream," said Nell.

"Can I play video games?" asked Eric.

"Let's play another tally game," said Dad.

"We can't count cars here," said Bridget. "Let's do T-shirts."

"Yellow!" called Eric.

"Green!" called Bridget.

"Red!" called Nell.

Eric laughed. "Red never wins," he said.

The line moved forward an inch at a time. They counted every T-shirt they could see.

21

"It's almost our turn," said Dad.
"Game's over. Add up your marks."

"I win!" Bridget shouted.

Mom took the shamrock medal from
Eric and placed it around Bridget's neck.

"You won't have the tally medal for long,"
said Eric.

"Oh yeah, Tally O'Malley?" Bridget replied.

Everyone was full after lunch. Eric, Bridget, and Nell slept most of the rest of the way to the beach.

Finally they arrived. They had just gotten out of the car when they heard a train whistle in the distance.

"Let's count the train cars," said Eric. "I pick the black ones."

"I take gray," said Bridget. "Do you want red again, Nell?"

"Yes," said Nell. "It's my favorite."

"You never learn," said Eric.

"There's the engine," said Eric. "It's black. One for me."

"No fair," said Bridget. "An engine's not a car."

A red car went by. Then another. Then another.

The next car was red, too. And the next one.

The train rattled past. Finally the caboose went by.

It was red.

"There were hardly any black cars," said Eric.

"Or gray cars, either," said Bridget.

"Let's see those tally sheets," said Mom. "Nell wins!"

Bridget handed the shamrock medal to Nell.

Then she noticed a sign near the tracks.

"Look at that!" she said. "That's why Nell won!"

travel THE
RED line

"Hey, Nell, that's not fair," said Eric.
"It seems fair to me," said Nell. "So from now on I want you to call me . . ."

Tally O'Malley!

In *Tally O'Malley*, the math concept is tallying. Tally marks are a useful tool for children as they learn how to keep track of objects they are counting and data collected over time. Grouping the tally marks also reinforces the ability to count by fives.

If you would like to have more fun with the math concepts presented in *Tally O'Malley*, here are a few suggestions:

- As you read the story, point out how the characters use tally marks to keep track of how many cars, T-shirts, and train cars they count. Point out how the diagonal tally mark is used to show a group of five tally marks.

- Reread the story and have the child keep track of the data with his or her own tally marks. Stop as you are reading and have the child compare those tally marks with the marks in the book. Make and complete a chart similar to the one shown here.

Name	Color	Tally Marks
Eric	silver cars	
Bridget	blue cars	
Nell	red cars	

- Have the child list the characters' names on a piece of paper and then tally the number of times each name is mentioned in the story. After the child is done tallying, ask questions like, "Which character was mentioned most often?" "Least often?"

- Say a number between 10 and 25. Have the child make tally marks to represent that number.